Columbus Day

Celebrating a Famous Explorer

Elaine Landau

Enslow Publishers, Inc.

40 Industrial Road   PO Box 38
Box 398   Aldershot
Berkeley Heights, NJ 07922   Hants GU12 6BP
USA   UK

http://www.enslow.com

For Aaron Herschberg

Library of Congress Cataloging-in-Publication Data

Landau, Elaine.
    Columbus Day : celebrating a famous explorer / Elaine Landau.
        p. cm. — (Finding out about holidays)
Includes bibliographical references and index.
ISBN 0-7660-1573-4
1. Columbus Day—Juvenile literature. 2. Columbus, Christopher—Juvenile literature.
3. America—Discovery and exploration—Spanish—Juvenile literature. [1. Columbus Day.
2. Columbus, Christopher. 3. Explorers. 4. America—Discovery and exploration—Spanish.
5. Holidays.] I. Title II. Series.
E120 .L26 2001
394.264—dc21
            00-010010

Printed in the United States of America

10 9 8 7 6 5 4 3 2

To Our Readers: We have done our best to make sure all Internet addresses in this book were active and appropriate when we went to press. However, the author and the publisher have no control over and assume no liability for the material available on those Internet sites or on other Web sites they may link to. Any comments or suggestions can be sent by e-mail to comments@enslow.com or to the address on the back cover.

Photo Credits: American Stock/Archive Photos, p. 20 (bottom); Archive Photos, pp. 4, 8, 15, 16, 18 (both), 20 (top and middle), 25, 26, 27, 28, 29, 30, 31, 32, 33, 34, 36, 38, 40, 45, 46, 47; Corel Corporation, pp. 41, 42, 44; Enslow Publishers, Inc., pp. 6, 10, 11, 19, 23; Hemera Technologies Inc., 1997–2000, pp. 1, 2, 3, 5, 7, 9, 13, 14; Hirz/Archive Photos, p. 22; Illustration courtesy of Skyler McGene, p. 12; John Crino/Archive Photos, p. 24; Lambert/Archive Photos, pp. 21, 37; National Aeronautics and Space Administration (NASA), p. 43; Reuters/Desmond Boylan/Archive Photos, p. 39.

Cover Photo: Archive Photos (main); Hemera Technologies and Corel Corporation (boxed images). Christopher Columbus (middle) is shown with two unidentified men from his mission.

CONTENTS

Christopher Columbus is famous for crossing the Atlantic Ocean by ship to reach the Americas.

CHAPTER 1

Christopher Columbus

When Christopher Columbus left from Europe, he was looking for a way to get to Asia by sea. He hoped to bring back some of the new and exciting things from Asia.

Hundreds of years ago a man from Genoa, Italy, dreamed of sailing to an unknown place. That man was Christopher Columbus.

Columbus is famous for crossing the Atlantic Ocean by ship to reach the Americas. This was a whole new world that people in Europe did not know about. But Columbus had not really hoped to find that part of the world. When he left Europe, he was looking for a way to get to Asia by sea. There were many new and exciting things in Asia. Columbus hoped to bring back some of them when he returned home.

Instead of reaching Asia, Columbus landed on an island in the Caribbean Sea that is now one of the islands of the West Indies. Columbus traveled to the New World four times between 1492 and 1504 to explore the West Indies. He also explored the coasts of Central America and South America.

Some people think that Columbus

The Americas were a whole new world that people in Europe did not know about.

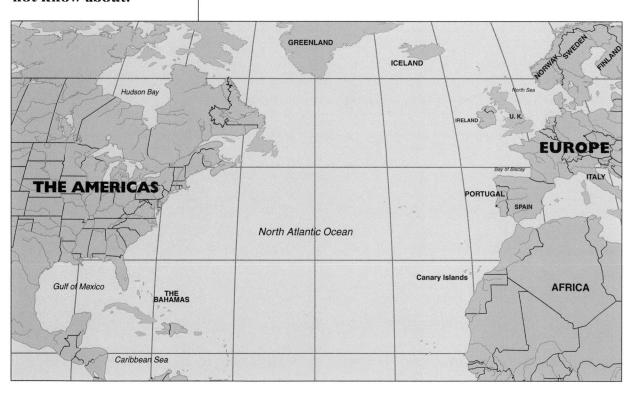

discovered America, but this is not quite true. The American Indians living there had arrived many years earlier. Columbus was not even the first European to sail there. In about A.D. 1000, Viking adventurers landed on the coast of North America. But they did not stay very long. The Vikings lived in the area that is now Denmark, Norway, and Sweden.

The Vikings came to North America in sailing ships like this one.

Columbus's trips led to a lasting link between Europe and the Americas. In time, other explorers followed, and trade and colonies grew. People's lives on both sides of the Atlantic Ocean were forever changed, and Christopher Columbus earned a place in history.

We remember Christopher Columbus each year on the second Monday in October. That is because Columbus landed in the West Indies on October 12, 1492.

Christopher Columbus was born in 1451 in Genoa, Italy.

CHAPTER 2

In the Beginning

C hristopher Columbus was born in 1451 in Genoa, Italy, a busy seaport on Italy's northwest coast.

We call him Christopher Columbus, but that is not what his parents called him. They named their child Christoforo Colombo. That is his name in Italian. Later, Columbus would go to Spain where he would be known as Cristobal Colón. That is his name in Spanish.

We do not know very much about Columbus's childhood, but we do know Columbus had four brothers and sisters. He was especially close to his brothers Bartholomew and Diego. They

No one really ever thought that Christopher Columbus would someday become a famous explorer. His father and grandfather were wool weavers. But his father wanted his eldest son to do more. He hoped that Christopher would someday become a very important businessman.

Genoa, Italy, is a busy seaport on Italy's northwest coast.

played together when they were children. As adults, they would often work together.

Trading was a successful business in Genoa. Many traders in Genoa made a great deal of money. They traveled to distant lands where they bought and sold many different things.

Columbus might have been a successful trader. As a boy he studied math and a language called Latin. Later, he wanted to do many things. But it took a lot of money to become a trader. So, at first, Columbus worked for a man who was a trader.

By the 1470s, Columbus had gone on several trading trips. He went to France in Europe, Tunisia in Africa, and other countries. He learned about trading and he also learned about sailing. He liked sailing the best.

Columbus moved from Italy to Portugal in

1476. We are not sure why he moved. According to the story, he was trying to get to England when pirates attacked his ship near Portugal. Columbus may have been hurt.

Christopher Columbus was not alone once he got to Portugal. His brother Bartholomew was there. Like Christopher, Bartholomew Columbus loved sea travel. Bartholomew and Christopher Columbus designed and sold maps to traders.

The Columbus brothers lived in Lisbon, Portugal, a very busy seaport. Ships were always coming into Lisbon. There were many chances to sail to distant places. Christopher Columbus sometimes sailed to those places.

In 1476, Columbus moved from Italy to Portugal.

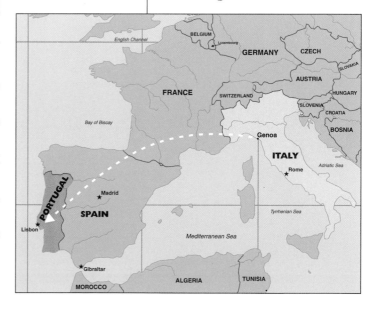

He did other things, too. He married a young woman named Felipa Perestrello de Moniz in 1479. A year later they had a son they named Diego. Felipa's father was governor of Porto Santo, a Portuguese island off the coast of northern Africa. Columbus lived there with his wife and child for a while.

In the early 1480s, Columbus sailed to the Canary Islands. This is a group of islands off the Western coast of Africa. He also visited West Africa. There he learned about the trade in slaves, gold, and gems like diamonds.

Columbus knew that what European traders needed most was a safe and shorter route to Asia. That was where India, Japan, China, and the East Indies were. These countries had gold, silk, and spices. Spices, like cloves and nutmeg, were not only put in food. They were

Columbus married Felipa Perestrello de Moniz in 1479.

also used as medicines, and people paid a lot of money for them.

But Asia was extremely hard to get to. It was a long and costly trip by land. Travelers were often attacked by bandits along the way.

It was not an easy sea voyage either. Sailors reached Asia in a roundabout way. They sailed south and then east around Africa. The passage was difficult and dangerous. Many ships were wrecked in storms at sea. Pirates sometimes attacked these vessels. The pirates knew that the ships carried valuable things.

Columbus studied all his maps and charts. Finally he came up with a new route to Asia. He wanted to sail west rather than east. Columbus thought this would shorten the trip.

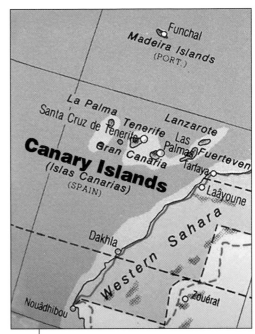

In the early 1480s, Columbus sailed from his home in Portugal to the Canary Islands. This group of islands is off the western coast of Africa.

Gold, spices, silks and other riches came from Asia.

After all, the earth is round. So sailors should be able to get to Asia from either direction.

At first no one believed Columbus. Some people think Columbus was not believed because he said the earth was round. That is not true. Smart people already knew that the earth was round. People did not believe Columbus for another reason.

Columbus thought the world was smaller than it was. That made him sure that Asia was much closer to Europe than it really was. There were other problems with Columbus's plan, too. The earth is covered with mostly water. But Columbus's maps showed it was covered with mostly land. He believed that Asia stretched farther east than it does.

Columbus also thought sailing west was the best way to go. That was wrong, too. Two large bodies of land blocked his path. Those areas of land were North and South America. Columbus did not know anything about these continents. Many years before, Viking explorer Leif Eriksson had landed in North America, but he had not realized where he was. And his people never settled the land. To Columbus, it was still new territory that had never been explored.

Christopher Columbus wished to try out his new route. But he needed people to help pay for the costly voyage. He had to have at least three ships to carry enough food, water, and supplies for a long trip. First he had to make others believe that he was right.

Today we know that Columbus never reached Asia. Instead, he found something far more valuable.

Many years before Columbus's voyage, Viking explorer Leif Eriksson had landed in North America.

Christopher Columbus is shown on the deck of his ship at sea.

"Full oft upon the deck

CHAPTER 3

Making the Dream Come True

A total of ninety men were onboard Columbus's three ships, including two of his brothers, Bartholomew and Diego. Most of the men were sailors. However, each ship also had a doctor. There was also a bookkeeper to keep track of the supplies, as well as a translator. Columbus had to be able to talk to the people in Asia, and he did not know how to speak their languages.

Christopher Columbus was determined to prove his ideas. In 1483 he met with King John II of Portugal. Columbus hoped the king would help pay for his voyage. But the king turned Columbus down. The king was sure Columbus would never reach Asia. Columbus still believed he could. He refused to give up.

The years ahead were difficult for Columbus. Many people laughed at his ideas. His wife died sometime between 1484 and 1485. Discouraged,

In 1486, Columbus went before King Ferdinand and Queen Isabella of Spain. He asked if they would help pay for his voyage to Asia.

Columbus left Portugal with his son, Diego, and went to Spain.

In 1486, Columbus went before King Ferdinand and Queen Isabella of Spain. He asked them if they would help pay for his voyage to Asia. The queen liked Columbus. She also liked the idea of finding a faster way to get to Asia. Yet, her advisers told her it was impossible. They realized that the world was larger than Columbus thought it was. They also knew that the earth had more water than land. Once again, the royal advisers were right. And, as before, Columbus did not believe them.

This time he was luckier. Queen Isabella was not quite convinced that Columbus was wrong. One other person advising the queen thought Columbus might be right. That person was the royal treasurer, Luís de Santangel. At the time, Spain did not have enough money to help pay for Columbus's voyage. However, the queen did not definitely say Spain would refuse to help.

Columbus waited and hoped. He continued to talk to the queen about the trip. He also looked for other people who could help pay for the trip. He went back to Portugal to ask King

Queen Isabella of Spain (sitting at left) listens as Columbus (standing at right) speaks.

Columbus had three ships for his voyage, the *Niña* (top), the *Pinta* (middle), and the *Santa María* (bottom).

John II again for help, but the king still refused. Columbus asked his brother Bartholomew to help. Bartholomew traveled to different countries looking for people who would be willing to help pay for the trip. He was turned down in both England and France.

Then in the spring of 1492 things changed. Spain had won a war. Now it had money for Columbus's voyage. Some people think that Queen Isabella sold her jewels to help, but that never happened. Luís de Santangel urged the queen to help pay for Columbus's voyage, and she took his advice.

Columbus excitedly prepared for the voyage. He had three ships—the *Niña*, the *Pinta* and the *Santa María*. Columbus was captain of the *Santa María*, the largest ship.

Columbus and his crew left from Spain on August 3, 1492.

But his favorite ship was the *Niña*. It was lighter and faster than the other two ships.

The wooden ships were not like the modern ships of today. Back then, ships did not have engines. So the crew had to move the ships using ropes and sails. Only the officers had

21

The *Santa María* is shown on the water.

sleeping quarters. The sailors found places to sleep on the open deck. In bad weather they slept down below. The food was not the best either. The men ate salty meat or fish and hard biscuits. They drank wine mixed with water.

On August 3, 1492, Columbus's three ships left Palos, Spain. The first stop was the Canary Islands. There the ships would be stocked with fresh food, water, and wood. The wood was used to do some repair work on the *Pinta*. The *Niña*'s sails were replaced with stronger ones.

On September 6 the voyage continued. At first the crew felt lucky. The winds were strong and in their favor. The ships made good time. But after about a month things changed. The men wondered why they had not reached land yet.

Fear spread among the men on the three ships. All had heard stories about horrible sea monsters. Now they wondered if these stories could be true. Many felt they would never reach Asia. And they were afraid of running out of food and water.

The men did not fight Columbus. But Columbus knew they were close to it. If that

All of the men on Columbus's ships had heard stories about horrible sea monsters.

23

Columbus and his crew finally spotted land in the distance on October 12, 1492.

happened, he might be thrown overboard. So Columbus made a bargain with his crew. He asked them to give him a few more days. If they did not reach land, he would turn the ships around. We will never know if Columbus would have kept his word.

Hopeful signs began to appear soon after Columbus spoke with his crew. Land birds were seen flying overhead. A tree branch was spotted in the water. Someone saw a large piece of wood in the sea. It looked as though it had been carved. Land was near, and it was finally spotted on October 12, 1492. The men celebrated by firing cannons into the air.

When they reached land, Columbus and his men got off the ships to explore.

Columbus thought his dream had come true. He dressed in his finest clothes to leave the ship and explore the land. He was sure he was in the East Indies. He could not have been more wrong. Once again, he did not know it.

Christopher Columbus (holding flag) and his crew finally reached land.

CHAPTER 4
The New World

Christopher Columbus was nowhere near Asia. He was in the West Indies. These islands are just southeast of Florida on the east coast of the United States. The native people there were farmers. They grew their own food and wove cloth. They lived in peaceful villages. Columbus called the native people Indians because he thought he was in the East Indies.

The Indians helped the visitors. They gave Columbus and his men food. They offered the men shelter and showed them the island. But their kindness was not returned.

Columbus and his crew landed in the West Indies. These islands are just southeast of Florida on the East Coast of the United States.

In time, Columbus and his men mistreated the Indians. They made them work long hours and gave them little food. If the Indians disobeyed, they were harshly punished. Many died from the lack of food and the cruel treatment they received. Some Indians died of diseases the Europeans brought with them.

Columbus had also brought Christianity to the Indians. He thought that this made up for what the Indians lost, but he was wrong.

Columbus wanted to explore the entire area. He still believed he was in Asia. He forced some of the Indians onto his ship to serve as guides. He also hoped to bring them back to Spain to impress the king and queen.

Columbus left some of his men on the island and set sail with the others. His next stop was the northern coast of the island of Hispaniola. Columbus took control of it and claimed it for Spain. He also traveled to Cuba. He thought it might be Japan. In Cuba he found a small amount of gold.

Columbus continued his travels. He hoped to find China before returning to

In 1492, Christopher Columbus met with the natives of San Salvador in Central America.

Christopher Columbus stands on the deck of one of his ships.

Spain, but his plans were cut short. On Christmas Eve Columbus went to bed early. A sailor was told to remain at the ship's wheel, to keep it on course. He did not; he ordered a cabin boy to do so instead. The young boy crashed the ship into dry land. The *Santa María* was wrecked on a reef near Haiti.

In a shipwreck much like this one, the *Santa María* crashed and was wrecked.

Once again the native people on the island helped Columbus. The explorer left about forty of his men in Haiti to build a fort and search for gold. The *Santa María* could not be repaired, so Columbus abandoned the ship.

The *Niña* and *Pinta* headed for Spain. The trip was extremely difficult. Some of the

Indians on the ships died. And there were terrible storms at sea.

When he got to Spain, Columbus was treated like a king. There were feasts in his honor. King Ferdinand and Queen Isabella gave Columbus an official title. He was now

Columbus was treated like a king when he returned to Spain from his voyage.

"Admiral of the Ocean Seas and Viceroy of the Indies."

The king and queen also ordered a second voyage to the New World. That would not be Columbus's last trip. In all, Columbus made four trips there. He explored the islands of Puerto Rico, Trinidad, and Jamaica. He explored parts of Central America and South America as well.

Columbus never found the riches he dreamed of. He also had many disappointments and suffered many hardships before dying in 1506. By then, he knew there was no quick route to Asia. But he never realized one important thing: He had opened the door to a whole new world.

This map shows the route Columbus took on his trip through the Bahamas.

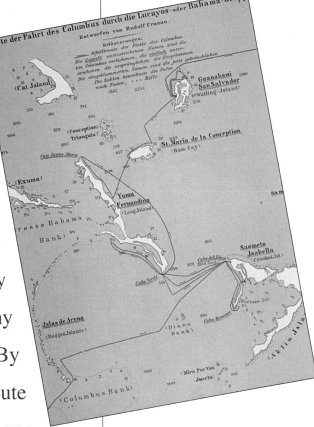

Christopher Columbus kneels before King Ferdinand and Queen Isabella of Spain.

CHAPTER 5
Remembering Columbus

One of the largest Columbus Day celebrations was called the World's Columbian Exposition. This was a fabulous world's fair in Chicago, Illinois. There were many interesting displays. These included actual-size models of Columbus's three ships. However, the fair required quite a bit of work. As a result, a whole year of preparations took place before the fair could open.

Christopher Columbus sailed to the New World. But we do not live in Columbia. We live in America. The continents of North and South America were not named for Columbus. They were named for another Italian explorer named Amerigo Vespucci.

Christopher Columbus was not forgotten. A South American country was named for him. It is the Republic of Colombia. The capital of the United States is Washington, D.C. The D.C. stands for District of Columbia. There is Columbus, Ohio, and Columbus, Georgia. Many

The continents of North America and South America are named after Amerigo Vespucci.

other cities, streets, schools, and buildings in the United States have Columbus's name.

There are also statues and monuments to honor Christopher Columbus. Paintings of him hang in many buildings. Often museums and libraries have exhibits about Columbus. Some trace his route to the Americas.

Yet, we did not always celebrate Columbus Day. The first official Columbus Day celebration was held on October 12, 1792. That was the three hundredth anniversary of Columbus's landing. A group known as the Society of St. Tammany, or the Colombian Order, planned it.

The idea did not catch on right away. There were only small celebrations in different parts of the country. Often Italian-American groups sponsored these gatherings. The Italian

Americans were proud that Columbus was Italian.

The next large Columbus Day celebration was in 1892. It was the four hundredth anniversary of Columbus's arrival. President Benjamin Harrison of the United States liked the idea. He asked Americans everywhere to celebrate. Schools put on shows about Columbus. Community centers had parties and dances. A ballet called *Columbus and the Discovery of America* was even written.

After 1892, Columbus Day was celebrated more regularly. Some people felt it should be an official holiday. They asked their state lawmakers to declare Columbus Day an official holiday. In 1909, New York became the first state to do so. On October 12 the governor

Statues, like this one in Philadelphia, Pennsylvania, remind us of what Columbus did.

led a grand parade. There have been Columbus Day parades in New York ever since.

There have been Columbus Day parades in other places as well. Many states also made Columbus Day a legal holiday. Usually a parade was part of the celebration. Finally, in 1971, Columbus Day became a federal holiday. This means that on October 12 all government offices are closed. There is no mail delivery. Many businesses and schools do not open. It is supposed to be a day of celebration in honor of Christopher Columbus.

Not everyone celebrates. American Indians do not feel that Columbus was a hero. They dislike the cruel treatment their people received from Columbus and his men. In some cities American Indians have protested

Columbus Day was not always a holiday. But, we have found many ways to honor Columbus since his famous voyage.

Columbus Day. They want to replace it with a different holiday that honors all Americans.

This new holiday is already celebrated in many Latin American countries. On October 12 those countries celebrate Día de la Raza (Day of the Race). This is a celebration of all people and of Columbus's voyages. There are usually parades, festivals, and speeches. In some cities in the United States things are changing, too. "Ethnic Diversity Day" has taken the place of Columbus Day activities in some areas.

This military parade honored Christopher Columbus in Spain on October 12, 1999.

Christopher Columbus's voyage helped people to see that the world was bigger than they thought.

CHAPTER 6

Celebrating Your Way

How is Columbus Day celebrated? Most towns and cities have parades. Some places do more. Farmingdale, Long Island, in New York, has an annual Columbus Weekend Fair. This includes a carnival, barbecue, and live music. Stores have sidewalk sales. There is a magic show for children, and the event ends with fireworks.

Columbus Day is fun on Jack Frost Mountain in Pennsylvania. There is an arts and crafts festival. Over seventy artists take part. You can ride a chairlift up the mountain. And there is always lots of good food.

Columbus Day is celebrated with fairs and carnivals in many towns across the United States.

The city of Columbus, Kansas, celebrates in a big way. It hosts a fun-filled three-day festival. There is a Miss Columbus pageant and a classic car show. People go for hot-air balloon rides.

Some groups in Berkeley, California, celebrate in a different way. They enjoy Indigenous People's Day. This is a celebration of American-Indian cultures. There are Indian-American dances, foods, and crafts.

The city of Columbus, Ohio, has been true to its name. It built a model of the *Santa*

María. Actors there play the parts of the people from the voyage. Visitors can meet the actors and see the inner workings of the ship. They can hear how cannon fire signaled the *Niña* or *Pinta*. It is the next best thing to sailing with Columbus.

Columbus Day is a good time to think about the past. But it is a good time to think about the future as well. Much has changed through the years. Today there are new frontiers to explore.

In the fifteenth century, people explored the sea and the land. Now we are exploring space. Would Columbus have wanted to visit Mars? Would he have come up with a shorter route to get there? Whole new universes await us. Perhaps you will be among those who help explore them.

Columbus explored the sea and the land. Now we are exploring space.

Columbus Day Craft Project

★

Sailboat

Christopher Columbus liked to sail. This project will show you how to make your own small boat. You will need:

✔ **a three-inch square of paper**

✔ **crayons or markers**

✔ **a toothpick**

✔ **a small piece of colored clay**

✔ **a walnut shell half**

❶ Decorate the paper square with the crayons or markers. Make it as colorful as you like. It will be the boat's sail.

❷ With the toothpick, poke two holes in the paper. Push the toothpick through one hole and out the other.

❸ Roll the colored clay into a ball. Place it firmly in the middle of the inside of the walnut shell.

❹ Stick the end of the toothpick in the colored clay. The sail should stand up straight. Now your boat is ready to float in the sink or in a bowl of water.

*Safety Note: Be sure to ask for help from an adult, if needed, to complete this project.

Words to Know

★

anniversary—The day each year when a past event is celebrated.

cargo—The goods carried by a ship, airplane, truck, or other vehicle.

continent—One of the seven large land areas on the earth.

explorer—A person who travels to unknown places.

native—A person who was born in the country in which he or she lives.

New World—The name sometimes used for North and South America.

territory—Any large area of land.

vessel—A ship, or large boat.

voyage—A trip by water or through space.

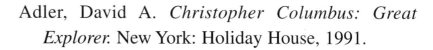

Reading About

★

Adler, David A. *Christopher Columbus: Great Explorer.* New York: Holiday House, 1991.

———. *A Picture Book of Christopher Columbus.* New York: Holiday House, 1991.

Clare, John D. editor. *The Voyage of Christopher Columbus.* San Diego: Harcourt Brace Jovanovich, 1992.

Dyson, John. *Westward With Columbus.* New York: Scholastic, 1991.

Fritz, Jean. *Where Do You Think You're Going, Christopher Columbus?* New York: Penguin Putnam Books for Young Readers, 1997.

Sis, Peter. *Follow the Dream: The Story of Christopher Columbus.* New York: Alfred A. Knopf, 1991.

Smith, Barry. *The First Voyage of Christopher Columbus: 1492.* New York: Viking Press, 1992.

Young, Robert. *Christopher Columbus and His Voyage to America.* Parsippany, N.J.: Silver Burdett Press, 1996.

Internet Addresses

★

COLUMBUS DAY FOR KIDS
<http://www.geocities.com/Athens/Acropolis/
1465/colprojects.html>

COLUMBUS DAY AT KID'S DOMAIN
<http://www.kidsdomain.com/holiday/
columbusday.html>

THE NEW YORK PUBLIC LIBRARY—
CELEBRATE COLUMBUS DAY!
A READING LIST FOR CHILDREN
<http://www.nypl.org/branch/kids/colon.html>

Index

★